Under the Snow

Written by **Melissa Stewart**
Illustrated by **Constance R. Bergum**

PEACHTREE
ATLANTA

In the heart of winter, a deep layer of snow blankets fields and forests, ponds and wetlands.

You spend your days sledding and skating
and having snowball fights.

But under the snow lies a hidden world.

Under the snow in a field…

…dozens of ladybugs pack
themselves into a gap in an
old stone wall.

Below them, a snake rests
in a hole all its own.

Voles spend their days
tunneling through the snow.

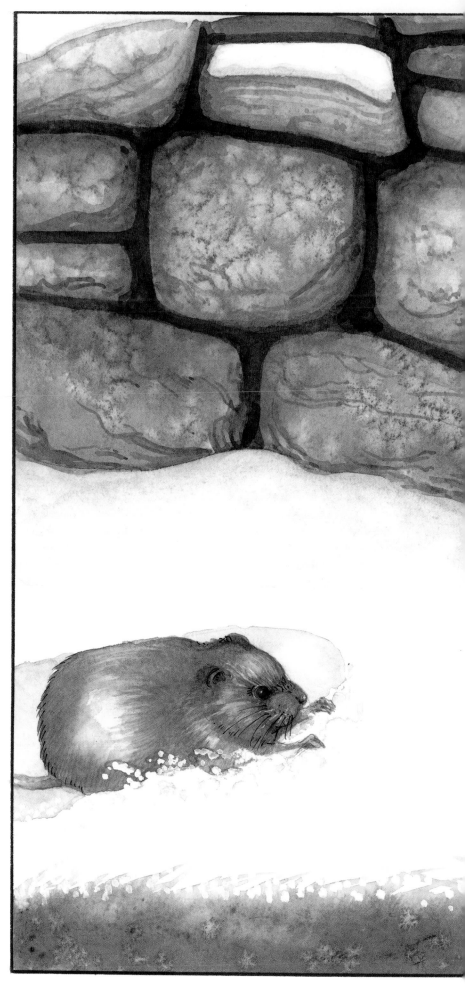

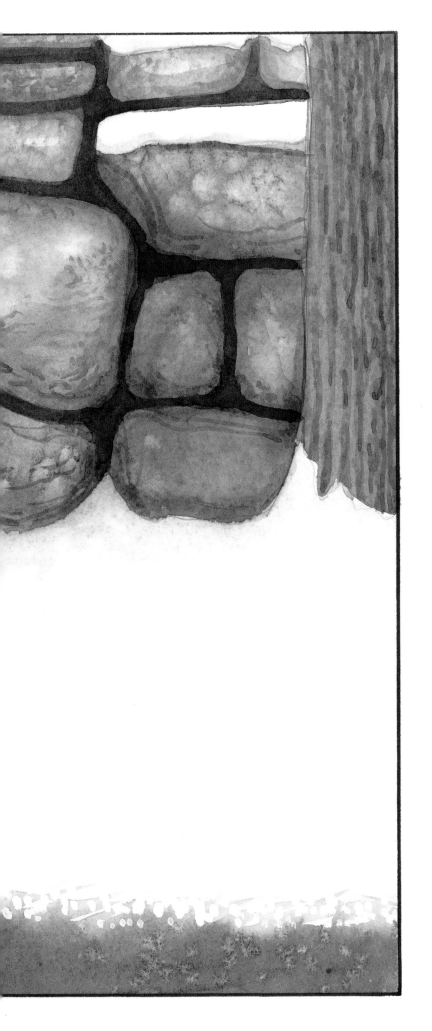

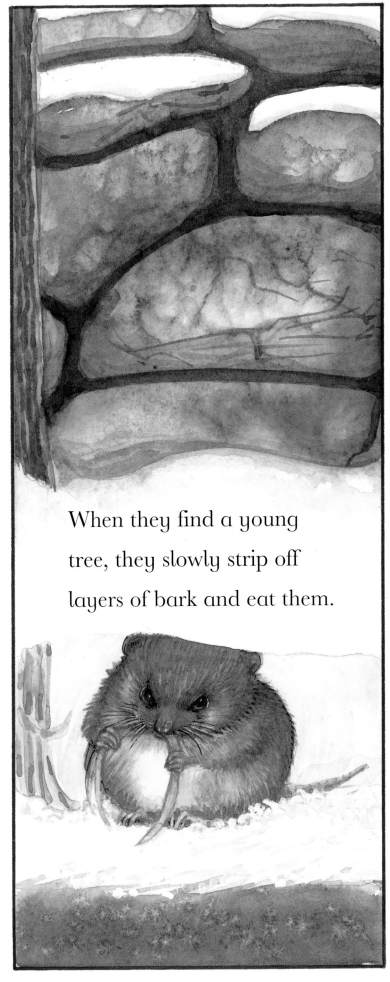

When they find a young
tree, they slowly strip off
layers of bark and eat them.

Below the ground, a chipmunk snoozes for a few days at a time. Between naps it snacks on the nuts and seeds stored in its burrow.

Under the snow in a forest…

…a mourning cloak butterfly
takes cover in a pile of brush.

Inside a rotting log,
a centipede and a
bumblebee queen
remain silent and
still until spring.

A wood frog nestles in scattered leaves on the forest floor.

It can freeze solid and still survive.

Not far away, a woolly bear caterpillar spends the winter curled up in a tight ball.

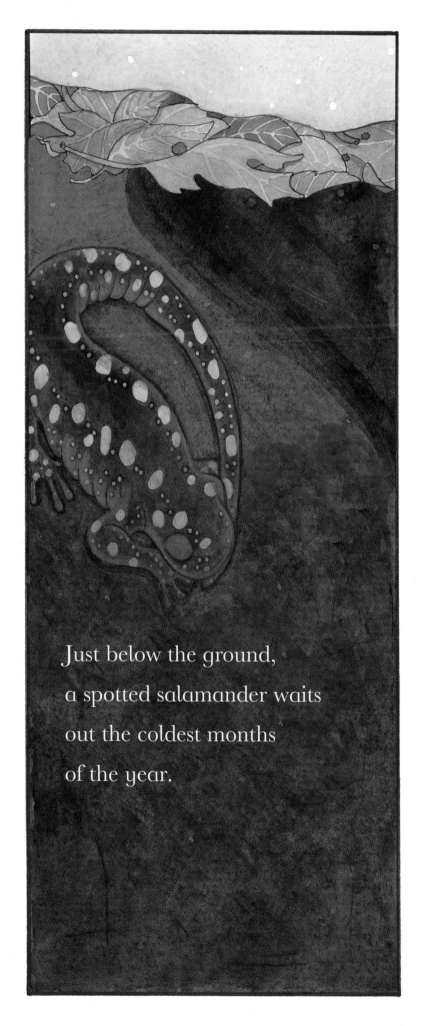

Just below the ground,
a spotted salamander waits
out the coldest months
of the year.

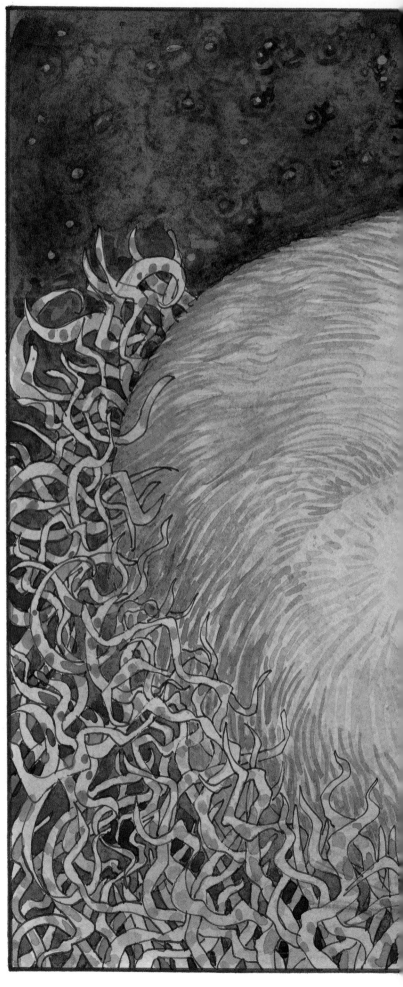

Deeper down, a woodchuck sleeps soundly all winter long.
Its heart rate drops and its breathing slows. The animal
gets all the energy it needs from its thick layer of fat.

Under the snow on a pond…

…bluegills circle slowly through the chilly water. They don't have enough energy to chase the waterboatmen swimming nearby.

A carp rests quietly
on the muddy bottom.

It isn't even tempted by the water striders lying just a few inches away.

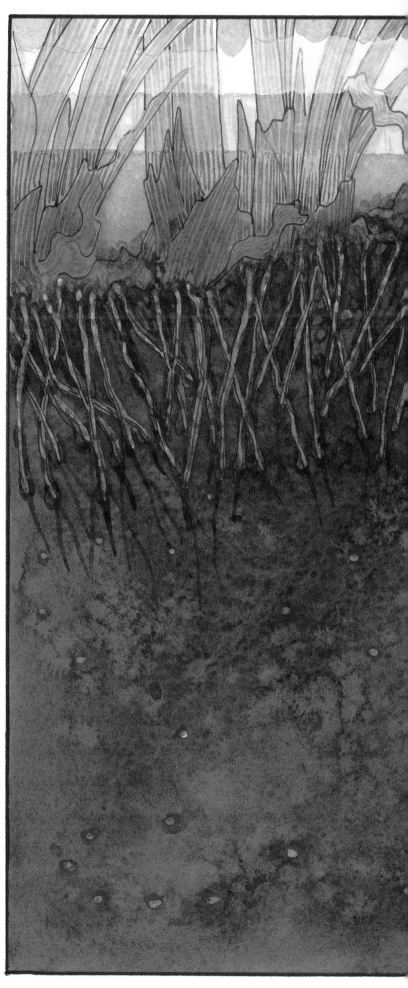

Buried in the mud, a frog and a turtle wait out the winter.
They never move, and they barely breathe.

Under the snow in a wetland...

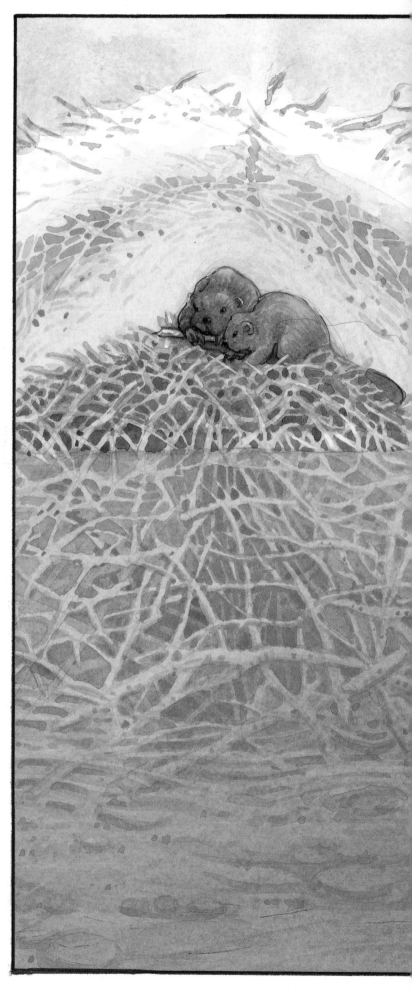

...a beaver family huddles together inside a cozy log lodge. When they get hungry, they swim to their food storage pile and munch on some sticks.

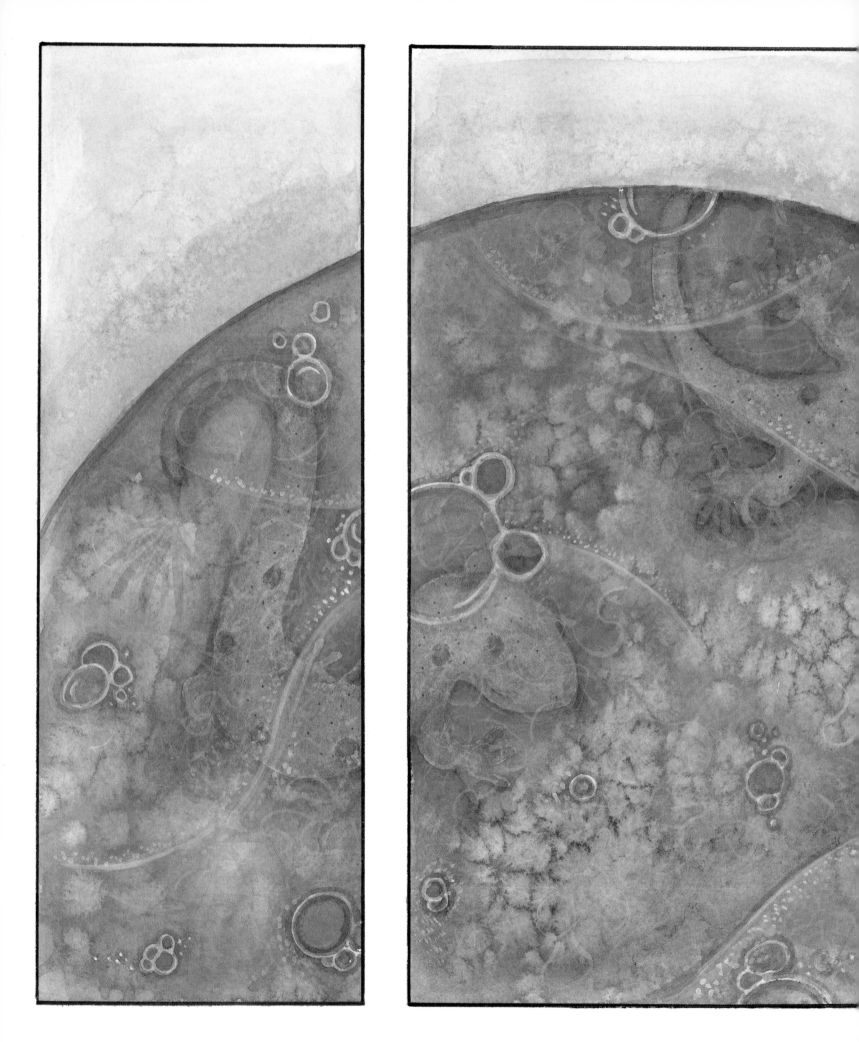

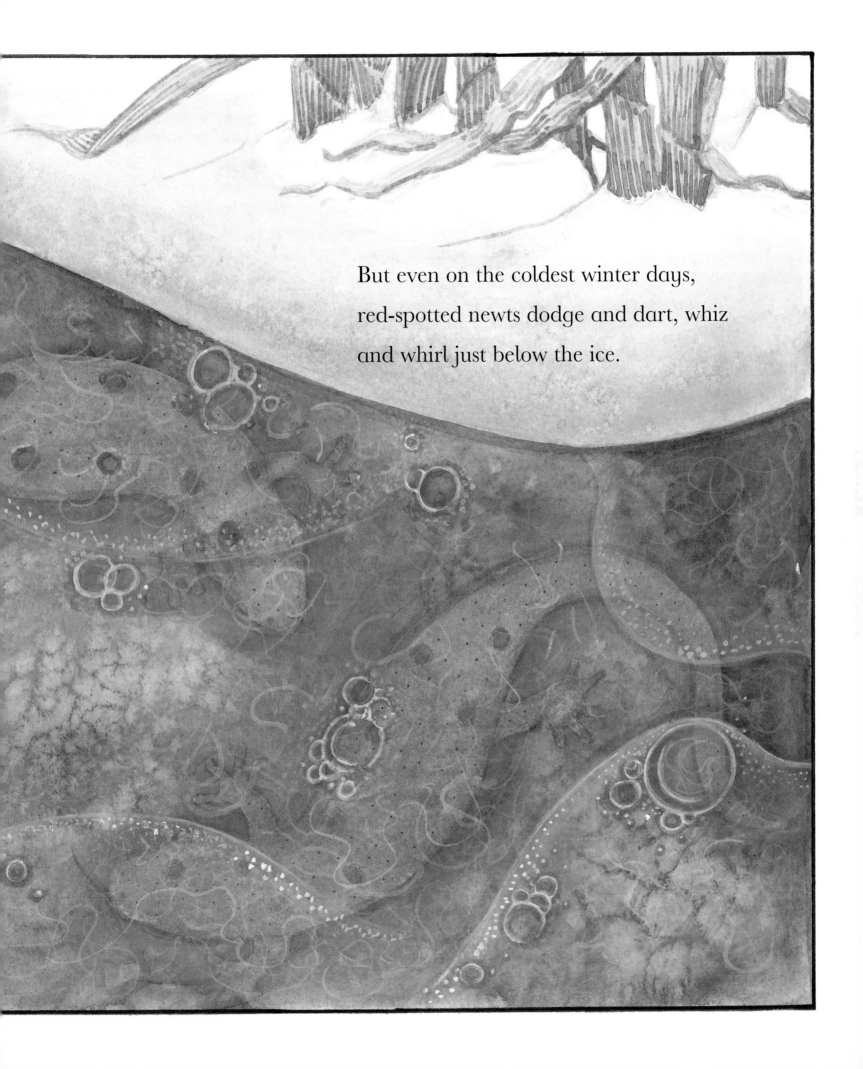

But even on the coldest winter days,
red-spotted newts dodge and dart, whiz
and whirl just below the ice.

As time passes, the sun's rays slowly grow
stronger. Each day is a little bit longer. Animals
living in fields and forests, ponds and wetlands
begin to get ready for spring.

And so do you.

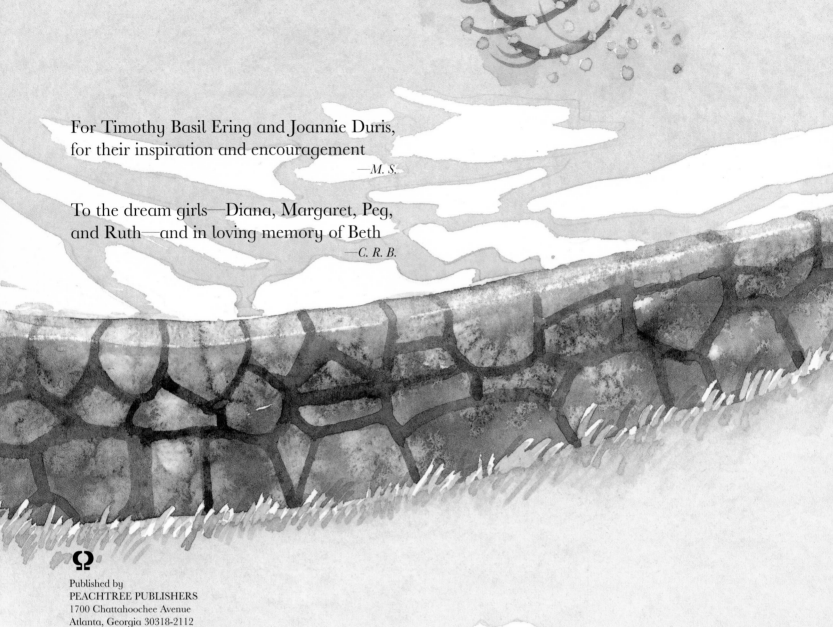

For Timothy Basil Ering and Joannie Duris,
for their inspiration and encouragement
—*M. S.*

To the dream girls—Diana, Margaret, Peg,
and Ruth—and in loving memory of Beth
—*C. R. B.*

Published by
PEACHTREE PUBLISHERS
1700 Chattahoochee Avenue
Atlanta, Georgia 30318-2112
www.peachtree-online.com

Text © 2009 by Melissa Stewart
Illustrations © 2009 by Constance R. Bergum

Illustrations created in watercolor on 100% rag watercolor paper; text typeset in Baskerville Infant
and title typeset in Linotype's Britannic Bold.

Book and cover design by Loraine M. Joyner
Composition by Melanie McMahon Ives

Printed in July 2010 by Imago in Singapore
10 9 8 7 6 5 4 3

Library of Congress Cataloging-in-Publication Data

Stewart, Melissa.
  Under the snow: written by Melissa Stewart ; illustrated by Constance R. Bergum.
    p. cm.
  ISBN 978-1-56145-493-8 / 1-56145-493-1
  1. Snow--Juvenile literature. I. Bergum, Constance Rummel, ill. II. Title.
  QC926.37.S76 2009
  591.4'3--dc22
                           2008052838